Give Yourself Time &
Trust The Universe

-a Collection of Inspiration-

Danielle Saeland

BookLeaf
Publishing

India | USA | UK

Made with ❤ on the BookLeaf Publishing Platform
www.bookleafpub.in
www.bookleafpub.com

Dedication

I dedicate this book to my three babies, my niece & nephew.
Because of all five of you-
Because of your smile, your laugh, your wild & free spirit..
Your kindness & gentle hearts..
Because of your natural abilities, to do just about everything..
The way you show me how to grieve, the way you leap over all obstacles life throws at you, the way you connect to a higher power, the way you look at life..
Because you show me how to embrace my inner child..
All of you have taught me how to truly love and how to live a life with purpose.
You all are my purpose.
Because of you, I choose to keep going.
I choose to rise from the ashes at rock bottom.
I choose to provide you with the most beautiful life we could ever imagine..
Because you all are alive-
I can be too.
Never stop being you.
Never stop being wild & free. Never stop loving with all your heart.

Never stop showing the world what you're made of.
Thank you, all five of you-
For being apart of my life.
I owe this book to all of you.

Cam
Kay
Mira
Layla
Kevi

Preface

It's been the worst year of my life.
The amount of loss my heart had to bare..
The amount of tears my eyes had to spare..
It was in these moments, I could only write.
My journal, with stickers & my bright colored pen-
I wrote it all out. From beginning to end.
I held my journal close,
It was only of a positive dose.
I wrote down anything that spoke to me,
They may not all be mine-but I let it be.
For each one, I could deeply feel,
In my journal, they went,
To help me truly heal.
It was these words, poems and more-
The inspiration I needed-
To finally close that door.

***

To anyone who has been through hell and back..
To anyone who has cried & cried..many sleepless nights..
To anyone who was been at their lowest point in life..
To anyone who has experienced love & loss..either
through divorce or death..or what feels like both at the

same time..
To anyone who thought they loved someone so
deeply..to be betrayed in the end..
To anyone who had to lay their best friend to rest..
To anyone who fought for their sanity..in the mist of the
darkness..
To anyone who felt ashamed or embarrassed about their
life circumstances..
To anyone who got crushed into a million pieces..
To anyone who was at rock bottom to only discover, the
fire had just began..
To anyone who became ashes laying on the ground..
To anyone who felt trapped in their own cocoon..
It's OK.
Life gets better..
Just hang on..pray, believe, have faith but most
importantly, please know..
YOU ARE ENOUGH.
It's ok to cry. It's ok to be mad, angry, frustrated &
confused.
Let it out.
FEEL IT.
Acknowledge it.
Trust that it will pass..
Then..when you feel you can finally stand up..
LET IT GO.
Rise up from those ashes..

Like the true Phoenix you are.

Transform into that beautiful butterfly..

Now it's time to spread your own wings & fly.

And always remember:

GIVE YOURSELF TIME & TRUST THE UNIVERSE!!

***

Acknowledgements

I want to say, to each & every one of you:
Thank You...

You held me up, when I was falling..
You made me smile, when all I could do, was cry.
You showed me a better way, every day.
You stayed strong, when I was weak.
You never stopped loving me, even after I pushed you away..
You took us in, with no questions asked..
You gave us a new home, your home.
You sacrificed your space and time, for us.
The love you showed us, what true family is..
For all the times you put up with me,
Even when, you didn't want to..
You stayed by my side, every step of the way.
When I thought I couldn't bare anymore..
You took on more, when all you wanted to do, was break..
For all the support, kindness and love..
I owe my new beginnings to all of you.
I thank each & every one of you..
Thank you for helping me rise from ashes..
Thank you for helping me break free from my cocoon..

For together, we will rise, to incredibly new heights!
Thank you.
Thank you, for being you.

My mom, my dad, my sister, my brother in law, my
nephew, my niece, my three kids, & last but not least; my
step mom, who became an angel on 9/12/24.

I love you all of you.
thank you.

1. Let Him Go

He was unbothered watching me lose my mind over his
destructive behaviours.
I lost myself and realized I was fighting for something
that was destroying me.
The truth is that he's broken and I wasn't meant to fix or
force him to get himself back together.
I healed and learned that how people treat you is a
reflection of how they feel about themselves and "what
you tolerate, you also encourage'.
Moral of the story:
Never let a person get comfortable with mistreating you.
What you tolerate today will be the same things that
imprison you tomorrow.
-unknown author

***

'I walked away because you were to busy finding faults
in me, while I was too busy overlooking yours'
Let that sink in.
-The modern breakup Novel

The Wisdom Of Letting Go
Be like a tree, and let the old leaves fall,
In their fading, find wisdom for us all.
To cling too tightly brings sorrow and pain,
But in letting go, there's so much to gain.
The past may weigh heavy, but it's not ours to keep,
Release it gently, and your soul will sleep deep.
Like branches stretching toward the sky,
We grow when we're unafraid to say goodbye.
For every leaf that drops, new buds appear,
Change is a cycle we needn't fear.
In shedding the weight of what's no longer true,
We make space for the light, for growth that's new.
Let go of regret, let go of fear,
In every ending, fresh beginnings are near.
Like the tree in winter, stripped bare and cold,
Know that in time, new stories unfold.
In life, we learn not all can remain,
But through each loss, we break free from the chain.
The winds may blow, the storms may roar,
Yet, by letting go, we stand even more.
Hold onto hope, not the things that must fade,
In this lesson, the path of peace is laid.
For the leaves that drop will nourish the ground,

And in their falling, true strength is found.
True strength lies not in holding on, but in knowing
when to let go. Life's beauty is found in accepting
change, embracing growth, and trusting that what's
meant for you will find its way.
-Mariam Meriam

***

Your not allowed to miss me-
After you did everything to make sure you lost me.
A hard reality check. A boundary drawn. A heart
protected.
You had your chance, you made your choice.
To push me away, to hear my voice.
To ignore my needs, disregard my feelings,
Left me no option but to distance and heal.
Now, don't come crawling back, with tears in your eyes.
Regretting what you had, and your goodbyes.
You can't miss what you didn't value.
What you carelessly discarded, like a fading ember.
You're not entitled to my presence,
After you tore our connection, leaving only silence.
You can't long for what you broke,
What you shattered, leaving my heart to ache.
Your actions had consequences,
Leaving me no choice but to move on.

I won't be your convenience,
Your safety net, your emotional crutch.
You had the opportunity to make it right.
But you choose to let me go, into the night.
Now, respect my boundaries,
And let me heal, without your guilt.
You're not allowed to miss me,
I'm moving forward, leaving the past.
Where you'll remain, with the memories that won't last.
Don't reach out, don't try to reconnect,
Your chance is gone, and I won't look back.
I've found my strength, my voice, my way,
And your just a memory, fading away.
This is closure. This is goodbye.
A chapter closed, a new life to apply.
You're not allowed to miss me,
Not after everything you did to lose me.
-unknown

***

Let him go.
He does not deserve to keep you.
-R. H Sin

***

The trees are about to show us, how lovely it is, to let the
dead things go.
5

***

Let him go, baby girl..
Let him go & move the HELL on.
-Unknown

2. The Law of Attraction

Whatever you put attention to will start to manifesting
in your life.
Intention, Attention, Manifesting; That is how the
Universe works.

***

You create your thoughts, your thoughts create your
intentions & your intentions create your reality.
-Dr. Wayne Dyer

***

Energy goes where intention goes.

***

Positive Mind.
Positive Vibes.
Positive Life.

***

I am a magnet for all that is good in this universe!

***

'Whether you think you can or can't, either way, you are
right.'
-Henry Ford

***

How to Manifest Your Dream Life:
'The Law of Attraction'
1. Visualize your dream life
2. Use affirmations to replace limiting beliefs
3. Have faith in the process
4. Math the frequency of the reality you want
5. Focus on the journey
6. Be purposeful with your thoughts & beliefs
7. Release control
8. What you focus on, the universe will work to help
   you achieve it
9. You are what you think, so carefully watch your
   thoughts

10. Find what makes you feel authentic & true to who you are
11. Align actions with your goals
12. Always trust your intuition

***

MANIFEST
Think it, Believe it, Write it down, Ask the Universe for it, Make it Happen

***

As you think, you feel.
As you feel, you radiate.
As you radiate, you create.

***

What you think,
You become.
What you feel,
You attract.
What you imagine,
You create.
-Buddha

***

Be mindful. Be grateful. Be positive. Be true. Be kind.

***

Take time to make your soul happy.

3. In Just 1 Day

We are born in 1 day. We die in 1 day. We can change in
1 day. We can fall in love in 1 day.
Anything can happen in just 1 day..

***

Maybe your path is harder because your calling is
higher..

***

There are losses that rearrange the world.
Deaths that change the way you see everything..
Grief that tears everything down.
Pain that transports you to a entirely different universe..
Even while everyone else thinks nothing has really
changed.
Megan Devine

***

It is both a blessing and a curse-
To feel everything so very deeply.

***

He showed me how to get lost. Then I showed myself
how to get found.
-Gayle Forman

***

One day-
I'll be at the place-
I always wanted to be.

***

One day or day one.
It's your decision.

***

One day at a time.

***

One day it will all make sense.

***

One day, it will all fall into place, and you will finally
understand why it had to be this way.

***

The sun rises & sets in just one day.
Breath..
The wind can change in just one day..
The leaves turn colors in just one day..
Let go.
This day will one day, be just another day.
Hold on..
Just one more day.
-Danielle Saeland

4. She Believed She Could, So She Did

They tell me 'it all happens for a reason'
And I gently cover the ears of the child within me then
whisper to her..
'You did not deserve this, and this is not your fault'
-unknown

***

She believed She Could-
So She Did

***

Be strong, my children.
Be brave. Be bold.
Be you.
Be free.
Be loved. Be happy.
Shine bright, my children.

Shine bright..
For you are-
My light.
Be you. Be Brave.
Be bold.
-Danielle Saeland

***

Six months from now, I want to look back at my life and say, 'You really did believe in yourself and it worked!'

***

She builds others up-
Because she knows what it's like to be torn down.

***

Unleash your inner child, be a little wild.
-Laura E. Brusseau

***

Be fearless in the pursuit of what sets your soul on fire.

***

Some days I'm a warrior.
Some days I'm a broken mess.
Most days I'm a bit of both.
But everyday I'm here.
Standing. Fighting. Trying.

5. Give Yourself Time

I am safe. I am at peace. I am free.
I am loved. I am thankful. I am blessed.
I trust the flow & process of life.
I trust in the universe.
I give myself time.
Time to change. Time to grow.
To start anew and to rebuild.
I let go of what no longer serves me.
I let go of the past. All my mistakes..
All my pain and all my negative thoughts.
I let the grave of God fill my heart.
I let myself feel. I embrace them.
I am whole. I am me.
-Danielle Saeland

***

The richest wealth is: Wisdom.
The strongest weapon is: Patience.
The greatest tonic is: Laughter.

& surprisly, all are free.

***

The meaning of life
Is to find your gift.
The purpose is life
Is to give it away.
Pablo Picasso

***

People Talk about Caterpillars becoming Butteries,
As though they just go into cocoon's,
Slap on wings and are good to go.
Caterpillars have to dissolve into a disgusting pile of goo,
To become butterflies.
So, if you are a mess right now, wrapped in blankets..
Just keep going.
Give Yourself Time.

6. Faith Can Move Mountains

Don't just learn- Experience.
Don't just read- Abosrb.
Don't just change- Transform.
Don't just relate- Advocate.
Don't just promise- Prove.
Don't just criticize- Encourage
Don't just think- Ponder
Don't just take- Give.
Don't just see- Feel.
Don't just dream- Do.
Don't just hear- Listen.
Don't just talk- Act.
Don't just tell-Show.
Don't just exist- Live.
-unknown

***

Ask for healing, clarity, peace, wisdom and guidance.

Ask for abundance, creativity, light & love.
Don't be timid in your prayers or your requests.
Be positive. Be grateful. Be bold.
Everything we are asking for-
Is already making its way to you.

***

Accept the present moment-
Exactly as it is.
Without wishing it was different.
This is the secret.

***

Your existence & purpose isn't random or by
coincidence.
You have many incredible gifts to offer that are just
waiting to be opened and spread to those around you.
Share often and deeply..
Someone's life is more meaningful & whole,
Simply because you're a big part of it.

***

When life knocks you down,

Roll over..
And look up at the stars!!

***

Learn to dance in the rain!!

***

Faith can move mountains!!

***

Don't worry about anything, instead pray about everything. Tell God what you need and thank him for all he has done.

7. Surrender to the Flow

You can't lose something you never had.

***

Your refusal to live a life
You don't want-
Should be stronger than
The fear of the unknown.

***

Always remember-
The words you most wish to hear from others,
Are the words you are at most of telling yourself..
You are beautiful.
You are loved.
You matter.
You are enough.
You are safe.
You are appreciated.

Forever & Always

***

Half of my life I tried to find peace
In the middle of the chaos.
Until I realized it's all about removing myself from the
chaos..
So that peace can truly find me.

***

Sometimes the blessing is not what the universe gives
you,
But what it takes away.
Surrender to the flow.
The universe is infinite wisdom and will provide you
with what you need.
Not necessarily what you want.
Trust it's wisdom.
Let go of what is not
Meant for you.

***

You have to resurrect the deep pain within you.
Give it a place to live that is not within your body.

Let it live in art. Let it live in writing, music.
Let it be devoured by building brighter connections.
Your body is not a coffin for your pain to be buried in.
Put it somewhere else.
-unknown

***

8. Stop Breaking Your Own Heart

Don't you see-
It's a trap.
If you keep trying to find everything..
You will wind up with
Nothing.

***

Stop breaking your own heart-
Trying to make a relationship work.
You can't force anyone to love you.
The truth is-
Sometimes the person you want-
Is the most love-
You would be better
Without.

***

Sometimes what comes into your life is not meant to
stay.
Don't lose yourself-
Fixing what never was meant to be.

***

It's better to be single-
Then to settle for less.
If you are seen as an option-
They don't deserve to be priority in yours.
Let go.

***

Don't let anyone,
Manipulate you into carrying the blame for their choices.
Your mistakes don't excuse their bad behavior.

9. 12 Laws of Karma

12 laws of Karma
***

The Great Law
Whatever energy & thoughts you put out into the
universe, you get back, bad or good.
***

The Law of Creaton
Life won't just happen to you. You need to take action
and make things happen. Rather than wait for
everything to magically work out for you.
***

The Law of Humility
Being humble enough to accept and understand that
your current situation is a result of your past actions.
***

The Law of Growth
Control yourself, not others and focus on your growth.
Personal growth as real change, starts with you.
***

The Law of Focus

Focus on one thing at a time and as long as your focus is on spiritual values, you won't have any greedy and negative thoughts.

***

The Law of Giving &,Hospitality
Give to the things you believe in from your heart. Understand and acknowledge that your actions are a reflection of your inherent beliefs.

***

The Law of Responsibilty
Whatever happens in your life, it happens because of you and you need to own it. You are the choices you make.

***

The Law of Connection
Your past, present and future, everything is connected. Your past actions determine who you are today and your present will decide who you will be tomorrow.

***

The Law of Here and Now
Living in the present moment is the only way to be truly happy. Holding on to the past and obsessing about the future will only make you unhappy.

***

The Law of Change
History keeps on repeating itself unless you learn your lesson and change your life. If you notice dramatic

changes it means you are growing.

***

The Law of Patience and Reward

Success requires patience, consistent hard work and the self assurance that you will get the rewards for your efforts.

***

The Law of Significane and Inspiration

Be it big or small, every contribution you make influences the universe. Your positive actions will bring more positivity into your life.

-unknown

10. Now Act Like It

Repeat every morning & before bed:
The universe always gives me everything I need.
I have motivation and virtuality.
I achieve my goals easily and quickly.
I have abundance.
I am grateful to the universe that my level of financial
freedom is growing every day.
I deserve all the best.
I am confident in myself and in my uniqueness.
I am perfect, and everything I touch becomes special.
All my intentions are eco friendly and successful.
I get everything I want, the best things happen to me.
-Danielle Saeland

***

Once you understand the power of your words,
You won't just say anything.
Once you understand the power of your thoughts,
You won't just think anything.

And once you understand the power of your presence,
You won't just be anywhere..
Know your worth
-unknown

***

How to feel better:
Angry = Sing.
Burnt out = Walk.
Overthinking = Write.
Anxious = Breathe.
Stressed = Exercise.
Sad = Gratitude.
Lazy = Cold shower.
Impatient = Reflect.

***

When you're nervous about stepping outside your
comfort zone, remind yourself:
'It feels scary because it's unfamiliar, not because I'm
incapable.'
-Michell C Clark

***

Our #1 job is to honor the goddess within.
Your secret self is the true Wonder Woman.
So, let her shine!
-Lynda Carter

***

P/S
You are Wonder Woman.
So act like it!

11. Either Way, We Win

That 'move' you are scared to make-
Just might be the
'One'
-Universe

***

Daily Motivation
Believe in yourself and all that you are.
Know that there is something inside you-
That is greater than any obstacle.

***

7 Things to master before the years ends:
Don't chase anyone.
Don't beg anyone to stay.
Know your worth.
Save space for people who matter
Accept what can't be changed

Leave what isn't for you
Love yourself

***

Going through things you never thought you would go
through..
Will take you to places you never thought you
Could get to.

***

Either my kids are going to see their mom,
Fully loved & respected by a man or,
They will see how she made the best life for us,
On her own.
Either way,
We win.
Period.

***

If you are serious about growth, be serious about:
Accountability
Time management
Good habits
Facing fears

Reading regularly
Networking
Saving money
Eating healthy
Exercising
Being open minded
Being focused
Trying new things
Never giving up
-unknown

***

The wrong people will always teach you the right
lessons.
-Book of Serenity

12. Bad Habit

It's like a bad habit to constantly want to reach out to
you.. to need you..to want you..
to only get rejected and made to feel like we had
nothing..
and made to think my experience of all the mess wasn't
real..
I can't keep doing this to myself .. I can't keep wanting
you..
I can't keep hoping you'll come back..
I've been through so much bullshit in my life..but this
year tops it..the pain of all the loss eats at me every day..
I've never had so much loss happen within such a short
time..
the up and down battle of grief is no joke..
I'm good for days, sometimes weeks..
then boom..like right now..
I'll I want to do is cry..and cry..
till I can't anymore..
I guess it's only time, that will heal me now.

The pain is so real-
how just one day can change everything..
one day everything is going so great-
your on cloud nine-
then..
the entire 'carpet rug' your flying on just drops to the
ground and shrivels to a million pieces..

I wasn't ready to lose my husband..
I wasn't ready to lose my house & my home..
I wasn't ready to lose my whole existence of the life I
loved..
I wasn't ready to lose my step mom..
I wasn't ready to say goodbye..
I wasn't done watching & admiring the healthiest
marriage I ever knew..
I wasn't done learning from her,
asking her questions and getting advice and
encouragement..
I wasn't ready..

But the universe has a funny way about it sometimes..
Sometimes it shakes you so hard and so fast..
You don't see it coming at all..
It's like, it has to slap you right in the face for you to
see..
to change and to grow..

My stepmother would always push me, just ever so
slightly, out of my comfort zone..
To help me achieve something I didn't know how to do
at almost 40 years old..
I wasn't ready to stop getting that from her..

I wasn't done needing her support as I go through the
hardest year of my life..
I wasn't done watching her get the perfect picture for
every holiday..
I wasn't done needing her.
I wasn't done talking to her..
I wasn't done smelling her amazing cooking..
I wasn't done..

I wasn't done being married.
I wasn't done having my husband as my best friend..
I wasn't done raising our kids together, like our parents
didn't..
I wasn't done needing him, by my side..
I wasn't done sharing my hopes & my dreams with him..
I wasn't done talking for hours about everything &
anything..
I wasn't done with my 'one person'..

But the universe has a funny how of showing you..
Just what you need, when you need it..

I wasn't happy anymore.
I wasn't moving forward with life.
It was stagnant.
I was pedaling backwards..
It was something I thought I wanted..
It was what I thought I needed..
But it was destroying me..
From the inside out..

Now, as I sit here, watching the sun go down..
Pretty colors-to nothing, but dark..
In the exact same spot I took you on date #2..
I can't help but think..
What is the universe trying to tell me now??
I'm trying so hard to hang on this crazy upside roller
coaster..without falling off, without falling flat on my
face..
My 'bad days' are shorter now.
Very far few & in between.
I'll take that and be grateful..
However, when the pain hits..
It hits hard.
Like a semi ran me over, chewed me up then spit me
out.. my whole body can't move..my mind can't
think..can't put two thoughts together..
it's just..mush..

I hate it when I get like this..
Because thats when I want to reach for my bad habit.
You...
Then I want to turn to you, once more..
Only to fall right back in the same cycle I was before..
Why is it so much harder to be happy, then to be sad or
mad..
I take 10 steps forward to get throw back 5..
I jump and leap and sometimes walk..
To be mentally slapped back to step 1..

I can't keep doing this to myself..
I can't keep wanting you..
I can't keep needing you..
I can't keep loving someone who doesn't exist..
But yet, here I am..needing you..

I miss your voice. I miss your comfort..
you always knew the perfect thing to say or do to snap
me back to you..
But where are you??
Some, 400+ miles away..
Being someone else, I don't even know anymore..
You say you need me. You say you want me..
Do you even know the 'me' you want anymore?

Please tell me the truth.

Can someone please wake me..shake me..anything!
This has to be a dream..
It just has to..

I need to drive home now.
Tuck the kids into bed..give goodnight kisses and see
their faces..

So farewell to the place, I once took you to..
So long ago..
Farewell to that life we lived together, for so long..
Farewell to you.
I wish you the best...I really do..
But most of all, someday I hope-
You pull your head outta your ass & wake up the fuck
up!
Someday you will see..
You just lost the best things in life, you ever had..
And when you come crawling back..
I'll just smile and say..
Fuck you!
I'm not looking back!
-Danielle Saeland

***

Sweetheart, the right guy will make you a priority.
If you find yourself feeling like you're not enough, it's
because he's not good enough.

***

You are overreacting.
No, you lied and I found out.

***

To change your life-
Change your habits

13. She's Not Coming Back

A man that loses a good woman will always feel a void
in his life.
I don't care what these weak red pill men have to say.
A man that loses his woman, because he's unable to
defeat his pride, ego, sexual desires and childhood
traumas, is lost!
You lost a woman who was truly loyal to you because
you couldn't battle the darkness within your mind!
You lost the only person who truly loved you because
you allowed a weak man to reach you that you were the
prize.
I don't give a dam about what a man has to say.
Love that woman or lose that woman or live a lifetime
with regret because when a good woman leaves you..
She's not coming back!!
-unknown

***

Shes not coming back.

A four word story for the boy
Who mistakenly thought she'd never
Realize her worth & walk away..
-Butterfly Rising

***

If you ever start to miss me,
Remember I didn't just walk away,
you let me go.

***

Sometimes the bravest thing you can do,
Is to never look back.

***

She's that woman-
The one you stay with or regret leaving.

***

If a man expects a woman to be his angel in life, he first
must create heaven for her.

14. Trust the Universe

Signs of High Vibration:
You feel grateful for what you have in your life
You are self-aware
You have a strong sense of empathy
You can better control your emotions
You are motivated to reaching your goals
You take care of yourself & wish to grow
You experience a lot of synchronicity
You feel connected to something greater than yourself
Your overall well-being is good, & you feel healthy.
You feel peaceful & stay away from srame
You feel confident & trust your instincts
You attract positive people
You feel happy
Your life feels meaningful
You smile & laugh more & have a great sense of humor
towards life
You listen to what your body needs
You live in the present, more than the past & future

***

'It's already yours!'
-Universe

***

Mindset is EVERYTHING.

***

The universe is not outside of you.
Look inside yourself;
Everything you want, you already are.
-Rumi

***

I rise from the ashes,
Transform out of my cocoon.
I give myself time.
I trust the universe.
I am a brand new butterfly-
A phoenix, born again.
I'm not looking back,
For now, I must fly..
And use my pain,
As my strength.

God bless you on your path-
Today, I say goodbye..
-Danielle Saeland

***

Trust your intuition.
They are love notes from the universe.

***

The universe has shaken you-
To awaken you.

15. I say Goodbye

Every ending-
Has a new beginning.

***

Sometimes letting things go-
Is an act of far greater power,
Than holding on.
-Eckhart Tolle

***

Tears water our growth.
-William Shakespeare

***

You can tell a person countless of times how they made you feel and they still won't get it if they don't intend to. You can clearly set your boundaries, emphasize the lines and what it costs if they cross it, but they still won't see

it if they're not putting an effort to look hard enough.
You can communicate well about how they make you
feel everytime they don't take your No's seriously and
they'll still forget it.
You can be fully honest with them about how you can
work it out or how you can meet halfway but they'll still
look past it.
You can explain your non-negotiables in detail, try your
best to be most considerate so you don't offend them, but
they'll hold it against you if they're not ready for a
confrontation.
Every time you try to communicate to people who aren't
ready to face their truths will just lead you to a loop of
avoidance and piling up of emotional baggages. Every
attempt to communicate will be misinterpreted as
starting an argument if you're doing it to the wrong
person.
You are not overreacting, you're not being petty. You're
being clear about your boundaries and you shouldn't be
sorry for it. You should actually be proud because not a
lot of people are brave enough to do that.
It's not you. It's just that you can't make yourself be
heard if they're not willing to listen.
You can't teach a wrong person how to treat you right.
-unknown author

***

Today I close the door to the past.
Open the door to the future.
Take a deep breath and step on through..
To start a new chapter, for my life.

***

Let it hurt.
Then let it go.
-R.H Sin

16. The Rise of a Woman

The Rise of a Woman
I wish I could see all the versions of myself that I once
was..
All lined up against the wall.
I would walk over to every single one of them and thank
them-
For not giving up...
When I knew they wanted to.
Your weakness is your strength.

***

She's not the princess
That needs saving..
She's the warrior
That needs a place
To rest between
Battles.

***

I am a warrior of light-
Shining bright.
Not afraid to take on this
Spiritual flight.

***

Theres nothing stronger,
Than a broken woman,
Who was rebuilt herself.
-Hannah Gadsby

***

On the days when your trauma is louder than your love,
just remember you are more than what has hurt you.

***

They whispered to her-
You can not with stand the storm.
She whispered back-
I am the storm.

***

I am as strong as Turkish coffee, I am magnificently wild,
I am chaotically beautiful, I am a goddess to be
cherished, I am fierce with an undeniable fire in my eyes,
and I am a free spirit. I don't need a man, I need a
goddamn warrior. A simple man just won't do!!
-unknown

***

Healing is so hard because it's a constant battle-
Between your inner child,
Who's scared and just wants safety..
Your inner teenager, who is angry and wants justice..
And your adult self.
Who is tired and just wants peace.
Be gentle with yourself.

17. Love Is

Love is patient.
Love is kind.
It does not envy.
It does not boast.
It is not proud.
It is not rude.
It is not self-seeking.
It is not easily angered.
It keeps no record of wrongs.
Love does not delight in evil but rejoices with the truth.
1 Corinthians 13:1

***

love is not what you say,
but what you do.

***

When love is unkind,
it is not love anymore.

***

When it comes to love-
Perfect is worth waiting for.
-Justin Blaney

***

Self love-
is not selfish.

***

Fall in love with your life.
Wake up early. Watch the sun rise.
Drink your favorite coffee.
Eat a good breakfast.
Get outside & go for a walk.
Go to the beach. Ride quads.
Watch the sun set.
Sleep under the stars.
Wear what makes you feel amazing.
Listen to your favorite music.
Dance as if no one is watching.
Sing at the top of your lungs!
Take a bath. Take a nap. Sleep in.

Make art. Color. Build something.
Do what makes your soul happy.
Purposely create those small moments.
So you can fall in love-
With yourself & your life.
Over & over, again!!
-Danielle Saeland

***

'Don't ignore the love you do have in your life by
focusing on the love you don't'
-Mandy Hale

***

And my last act of love-
Was leaving you alone,
So you could go do the things that hurt me- without me.

18. Spreads Seeds of Hope

I'm moving differently now, because I am different. I've
changed, l've grown, l've bloomed, I've leveled up. I
finally realized that access to me is a privilege.
My space doesn't have room for just anyone to come as
they please.
In the growing, through the dark, in all of my light, l've
learned to protect my peace.
I put in a change of address a long time ago, but this
time, I changed the address to my soul. If you reach me,
it's because I want you to.
- Stephanie Bennett-Henry

***

The Tao of the Dandelion
Bloom where you are planted
Yield to the wind
Find beauty in simplicity
Stand tall and be resilient
Don't be afraid to be different

Spread seeds of hope

***

H.O.P.E
Hold
On
Pain
Ends

***

Hope is the only thing-
Stronger than fear.

***

The darkest nights produce the brightest stars.

***

Only in the darkness can you see stars.
-Martin Luther King Jr

***

Faith. Hope. Love.

***

In case you haven't heard it today:
You are loved.
You are important.
You matter.
And you are, enough.

***

Let your light shine.

***

There's a crack in everything.
That's how the light gets in.
-leonard Cohen

19. That Girl

I'm that girl,
The one who skips on the beach
Dances in the rain
Sings in the shower
Howls at the moon
Gets lost in the woods,
Who prays by the fire.
I'm that girl,
The one who still hopes and dreams
Who has loved and lost
Who has crashed and burned
And risen from the ashes.
I'm that girl,
Who stopped talking and started doing
Who stopped settling
Who dared to believe in herself
Who lost all the filters,
and dared to expose her soul.
Yeah,
I'm that girl.

-Leslie Bertrand
Paradoxical Phoenix

***

I don't walk away to teach people a lesson.
I walked away because I learned mine.
I'd rather adjust my life to your absence than adjust my
boundaries to accommodate your disrespect.

***

You have spent enough time worrying about not being
enough in someone else's eyes.
Now it's time to be enough in your own.

***

She needed a hero.
So that's what she became.

***

Her soul is fierce.
Her heart is brave.
Her mind is strong.
-R.H Sin

***

The phoenix must burn to emerge.
-Janet Fitch

***

If you don't spread your wings,
You will not discover how far you can fly.
-Maltreya

***

Your wings already exist.
You just have to believe & fly.

20. Thank You

To the Man
Who I Once Thought to Be the Love of my Life.
Thank you for making me feel that I wasn't someone
worth fighting for.
Thank you for making me question and doubt every little
thing about myself.
Thank you for making me second guess my actions.
Thank you for making me feel unimportant and a
nuisance in your life.
Thank you for letting me down countless times.
Thank you for keeping secrets that made me feel that I
wasn't worth trusted for.
Thank you for constantly lying about who you really are.
Thank you for making a big fool out of me.
Thank you for bringing out my worst side.
Thank you for showing me that you can be completely
happy with someone else but not with me.
Thank you for leaving even if I give you everything I
had.
Thank you for letting go and reminding me that I was

the only one holding on.
Thank you for all the times you made me feel blue.
Thank you for making me believe that all the times I
spent loving you was infinite, but all was just an act.
Because if you hadn't done all these things, I wouldn't
realize my worth.
I wouldn't realize that I should finally stop settling for
any less than I deserve.
I wouldn't realize that I want to find a love that would
never make me feel the same things you did.
And I know I will, eventually.
I hope you know that I didn't quit, I just simply chose
myself instead of continuing to try for someone who
wouldn't try for me.
For now, knowing that is enough. I am enough.
I know I am, even if you didn't.
Thank you, Love.
Thank you.
-unknown

***

Life Tip:
Forget who forgets you.

***

When you choose to forgive those that hurt you, you take away their power.

***

Never let a man pull you low enough to hate him.
-Martin Luther King Jr

***

Never settle for less.

***

A weak man, can't handle a strong woman.

21. Everything is Art

You need 5 Hobbies:
One to make you money
One to keep you in shape
One to keep you creative
One to build knowledge
One to evolve your mind

***

Things That Count as Self-Care:
Taking a shower.
Reaching out to a friend.
Asking for space.
Going for a walk.
Reading a book.
Watching videos of baby animals.
Coffee.
Making something.
Telling the truth.
Napping.

Refusing to apologize for who you are and where you
are in your journey.

***

"I think everything in life is art. What you do. How you
dress. The way you love someone, and how you talk.
Your smile and your personality. What you believe in,
and all your dreams. The way you drink your tea.
How you decorate your home. Or party. Your grocery
list. The food you make. How your writing looks.
And the way you feel. Life is art."
-Helena Bonham Carter

***

"If you're not willing to do it in art, you're never gonna
do it in life."

***

" Mirror mirror on the wall I will always get up after I
fall.
Whether I run, I walk or I have to crawl.
I have set my goals and I will achieve them all ."
-unknown

***

The soul always knows what to do to heal itself-
The challenge is to silence the mind.
Silence it in writing.
Silence it in music.
Silence it is love.
Silence it in art.
Then..
Listen.

***

A girl with magic in her eyes
And a single paint brush,
That gave her all the colors she needed..
All the colors..
From her soul.
-Danielle Saeland

***

'Oh, darling- you are..'
'Just do art- in this -
Beautiful Chaos Life!'
-Danielle Saeland